a soft life

Your guide to living a high vibrational life.

the relaxed woman – a soft life

Copyright © 2024 the relaxed woman

a soft life

All rights reserved.

ISBN: 978-1-914275-99-9

Perspective Press Global Ltd

the relaxed woman – a soft life

إذن الى اين انت ذاهب

so where are you going?

And God says, 'so find me and I will fix your heart'.

the relaxed woman – a soft life

Your peace is your power. Your ability to breathe with ease, be mindful, and stay calm will make you the wealthiest person in the world. Often, the power of our minds is entirely misunderstood; the more you feed your mind, the more you learn, the wealthier you become. Making your mind the wealthiest asset you own is the best decision you will make. But keeping it calm in situations that are beyond your control will become your best trait.

In today's fast-paced world, traditional values have been lost, replaced by the opinions and corruption of modern society. While it's important to move with the times, as women, we've become less in tune with our femininity. We feel burnout much quicker and are consequently faced with more pressures from the outside world that don't necessarily align with our core beliefs and who we truly are.

When you truly master and understand that the world is merely a reflection of who you are and the state of your mind, you free yourself. You begin detangling from the expectations of the world and allow yourself to breathe. Your energy detaches itself from external forces, and you find peace from within, glowing from the inside out. Once you heal your mind and the things you feed it, you'll begin attracting compliments, flowing through life with ease, and seeing how the stars align to help everything flow in your favor.

the relaxed woman – a soft life

You were destined for all the beautiful things in life, and it's about time you begin remembering so. Once you rebuild your faith in the universe, you'll see how magnificently life begins to flow.

If you have these things, you are the richest; the richest in nature, in your innate being, in who you are at your core.

I think we can all agree 2023 was the year of lessons. It was a year of learning, losing ourselves, but we're here trying to find ourselves again. But we learned a lot during the process. My soft girl, this year you allowed people to treat you in a way you never thought you'd tolerate. You went from a place of 'I want to be liked by these people' to 'do I even like them'. You have grown - even if you don't see your growth, growth is happening. You learned why you would even want to be liked or validated by people you don't even respect. Or most importantly, why would you seek validation from those who don't have the same visions as you? I want you to start caring about the little girl inside of you. I want you to be extra mindful and to set your boundaries. How you choose to live your life is nobody else's business but yours. Going into the new year, I want you to realign yourself and remember who you are; I need you to remember your worth and what your place in this world is. God made you one of the highest-valued women, and it's about time you begin recognizing her again. I need you to remember the high-value woman you are. 2024 is the year you take back your power. You have such an incredible life in store for you, and I think you've lost sight of that lately. The universe adores you, my love; go and seek inspiration. Go and get a cup of coffee and remember who you are. Read, seek knowledge, allow yourself to glow from within. Take things easy and learn to embrace your soft life. The universe adores you, my love, all you have to do is look around.

Dedicated to the magnetic woman with endless potential at her fingertips – this is your world; you are capable of so much. Softness encompasses you; don't allow the corruptness of this world to make you into someone you're not. Stay grounded in your faith and continue to learn.

This book isn't just for those who are naturally soft; it's for anyone who's striving to rediscover their softer side, particularly in a world that's often overstimulating. Whether you're longing to reconnect with your inner self or aiming for personal growth, this book is your starting point, especially if you're unsure where to begin. In every setback, there is an opportunity; whatever breaks you also builds you. God has a reason for everything he does, a mission, a succinct plan behind everything. This idea of the 'soft girl era' has surfaced on social media, and I'm glad women are stepping into their femininity, but it's essential to remember that what you feed into yourself is just as important as your skincare regime. Discovering who you are at your core and stepping into your highest trajectory means much more. This book underscores the significance of nurturing your inner being. It's about delving deep into your core, understanding your essence, and wholeheartedly embracing it with patience and kindness, paving the way for a permanent embrace of your softest self. Think of this book as advice from your big sister: sure, you can indulge in external beauty treatments, but true contentment comes from within. You could feel like the most beautiful woman in the world, you can go for massages, facials, but if you're not content with who you are at your core, you'll constantly be wondering why you're struggling to find inner peace and clarity. This book walks alongside you on your journey towards embracing your best and softest self, gently reminding you that stumbling along the way is part of the journey and encouraging you to extend patience towards yourself. This book is your companion on the journey to your best and softest self, reminding you that it's okay to stumble along the way and urging you to be patient with yourself. In the midst of the 'soft girl era' trend on social media, it's easy to get caught up in external appearances. But this book emphasizes the importance of nourishing your inner self. It's about understanding who you are at your core and embracing your true essence with patience and kindness so you can embrace stepping into your softest self in its permanence.

To be soft requires patience; making patience your fundamental goal is your first step into embodying your kindest and calmest self. Patience is power - once you're patient, you embody your calm self. This is for the one who has been selfless for too long that her soul yearns to pour into herself - it's for the one who messes up sometimes but I wrote this to teach her that it's okay to mess up - this book is your reminder that it's okay to mess up while on your journey towards your softest self - you could have an amazing week of calmness, but if you have one day of agitation, you've lost sight of the amazing week you've had because you're so focused on the negative? Without the bad, there would be no good. Without the pressure, there would be no softness. Patience, as you'll discover, is a powerful tool for personal transformation. It's about challenging yourself to change your mindset and attitude while also giving yourself grace when things don't go as planned. If you've been putting others before yourself for too long, this book is your gentle reminder that it's okay to prioritize your own needs. It's okay to choose yourself for a while so you can come back to your softest self so you can pour into your loved ones. Embrace each day's challenges, knowing that every stumble is an opportunity for growth. You may be feeling sad right now, but every time you feel a certain way, you have the power to change how you feel, to become soft, to choose to be soft. It's going to take time. You know what you carry in your heart, and you know the power of your kindness. For the woman seeking her softest era, this book is your guide. It's for those who want to radiate purity, love, and kindness in all aspects of their lives and

the relaxed woman – a soft life

who are ready to embrace their truest selves with open arms.

May this year finally give you the inner peace you've been aimlessly searching for; may you walk through life trusting in His plan. You are destined to have it all, to accomplish it all; remember, everything you've ever wanted is already yours.

the relaxed woman – a soft life

Dear God, I am placing this year in your hands. You guide me, and I will follow you. And you, my angel, remember, 'heads or tails,' no matter how life may play out, you're always a winner in this game. Every path was laid out for you; your soul chooses the direction; your soul chooses the lessons it needs to learn no matter which way you go; you will always win. Their thoughts and opinions of you shouldn't cause a misalignment with who you are at your core. Knowing you are God's favorite and an effortless manifestor is enough to realize how blessed and favored you are.

If the previous few years have taught you anything, I hope you learned to be extra mindful with who you share information with; these people who hurt you were waiting for your downfall, so please be extra careful when you're sharing your goals or passions; there's a reason why they say stop telling your goals to people; their energy gets in the way of your manifestations; I don't care if it's your best friend, stop sharing your goals. Your visualizations and should remain between you, your creator, and your journal. Every time you tell people your goals - especially if these are people who don't share the same beliefs as you - they'll start sharing their limiting beliefs and questioning you on how you're capable. God knows how capable you are; he knows you were put here to do extraordinary things; he knows your purpose.

the relaxed woman – a soft life

Let them wonder what you're up to - keep doing your thing to make the world a better place, keep thriving, and continue being the authentic angel you are. Become the mysterious woman you've always wanted to be. Keep them in awe of your existence; for every time they see you, they don't even have the same access as they used to. You always come out on top – just as you always have. And to reach such a life comes with innate trust. Trust in yourself and that of the universe's power.

Sometimes we find ourselves in overstimulated environments, and it's okay to take time for yourself and breathe. She's in her world of comfort, knowing she is comforted by the universe, embracing her solitude, enjoying her own company, and feeding her mind with greatness. She's still trying to heal from the scars the external world has left on her, but she takes each day as it comes. Every day is a challenge on her journey of healing, but her intention for change is there; her desire to make herself greater is there. She's working on herself daily but also remaining soft to become the greatest version of her. And during this journey, she is tested by the world, but she continues to embrace her journey each day, enjoying and embracing her solo time. You'll often find her alone in her own company in the wonders of her mind - ready to see where the world will take her. Often misunderstood by those close to her - but she was never made to be average or to be understood.

Your internal dialogue is the one dialogue that is everlasting; the voice you will hear most in your lifetime. Make sure you treat it with kindness so you too can accept its kindness. And in his timing, I trust – the divinest of it all.

One thing I'm still learning is how we deal with circumstances that lead to our quality of life - and that's definitely a valuable lesson learned. Our minds can be our worst enemies sometimes, and the power of feeding positivity, especially during times of hardship, is one of the powerful tools you will ever acquire. The secret to life is how you deal with pain and situations beyond our control. And that's why faith is such a pivotal factor throughout every religion and life itself. Your knowing that all will work out, your knowing that things will work out just the way they always have is your superpower. That knowing that all is great. As I write this, I am still learning to surrender. I pray God remains patient with me. In Arabic, we have a saying called sabr - which literally translates to patience, and sabr is something I need, and I pray God remains patient with me.

Embrace this transition into your highest version of yourself. I want you to feel alive again. Stop allowing low vibrational energies interfere with yours; affirm with me 'I withdraw my energy from entities beyond me and return it to myself.' What people think of you doesn't take away from your worthiness from within; you are so respected and valued my love. All you have to do is look around and see how blessed you are.

Remember who you are. I think you've lost sight of your being lately. Who you are at your core. Don't ignore the beauty of what you have and who you are because others have made you feel a certain way. That's exactly what they want. For you to lose alignment with yourself, for you to forget who you are. Why are you forgetting your worth because of the opinions of others? When you are the embodiment of a soft woman, the opinion of others doesn't misalign you from your higher self because your purpose is greater. I want you to start living with purpose to begin seeing your life through the lens of the version of yourself that you visualize; being led to her purpose; being led with purpose, living through faith, and living her life through the lens of appreciation are her ultimate goals right now. And God whispered in her ear that all would be well; everything was aligning for her; the moment she breathed and took a step back, it would all fall into place. During this period of finding yourself, it'll be difficult when you've heard so many people who want to see you fail speak so negatively about you, but that's why your self-affirmations are important. It's so vital for you to spend time with yourself and for you to go where you are valued. Your solo time is your fuel time. Your time to devote and rebuild areas those who envy you have tried to break down. Your time to recharge and remember who you are without the validation from others.

You are not for everyone to understand, and that's okay. A woman like you wasn't made to fit into a room with ordinary people. Please stop feeling misaligned when you're not fitting in or if you feel a certain way. You just haven't found your room. Your soul strives for more; your purpose is greater, and you vibrate higher. You've just outgrown a lot of people. Outgrowing people means your journey will be a lonely one, but when you're a woman of God and you're devoted to following a Godly path, you realize your faith and your family (the family that comes from you) are all that you need. You have so much to give this world, and it's about time you begin realizing it. Your purity is at the heart of your soul. You've always been different because you've had more to give the world. Your desire to give back to this world is so immense it's not meant to be understood by small minds. And along your journey, there will be people who try and convince you what you're doing is 'crazy' and that what you're doing hasn't been done before, so please don't do it. But if you continue doing what's been done, you'll continue getting what you've always gotten. You're destined to break generational curses and make an impact, and I'm glad you're trusting in God's plan. Even when you don't understand, you trust. And that's exactly what God loves about you. I want you to remember that every time you feel misaligned or lost; I want you to remember who you are. Who you've been working so hard to become. Embrace your beautiful journey, my angel, because it's leading you exactly where you need to go. Remember, you're exactly where you need to be at this moment.

the relaxed woman – a soft life

As women, we are capable of magnificent things, but a truly feminine woman understands that her softness is her greatest asset. Please don't allow the corrupt influences of the modern world to lead you astray. Embracing your femininity and living a relaxed life will be one of your most powerful traits. While it's wonderful to witness your peers achieving success, it's crucial to ask yourself if that's the life you genuinely desire. If your heart's desire has always been to be a mother or to take care and invest in your home, why should someone who thrives in a masculine world daily deter you from your purpose? Of course, there lies greatness in wanting more for yourself, but you are doing so much just as you are. You are more than enough by simply being. At the end of the day, a truly feminine woman carries endless love within, and if being a wife is in your purpose, remember, the highest value man doesn't care what your career brings. He cares about what's in your heart. You have always had the power to make things happen. It's time to reclaim that power and remember who you are – the soft, unyielding woman who isn't swayed by external pressures. Being authentically you, without excessive effort, will take you to places you never thought possible. Amazing things unfold when you surrender and let go. In a society that idolizes hustle culture, practice being a relaxed woman. Embrace your feminine essence, for it is your femininity that attracts wonders beyond your imagination.

You want a soft life, but you don't know how to calm your mind. You want a soft life, but you fail to comply with the laws of the universe. You want a soft life, but you prioritize your business and those exterior to you over your inner well-being. The softest of women understand that complying with the laws of the universe and aligning yourself with your highest self is the best form of alliance with the universe. Please stop feeling guilty by seeing others scream about their success on social media. It's okay to work at your own pace and to work on your inner well-being.

Choosing to be a homemaker is just as commendable as climbing the corporate ladder. Please do not allow the influx of social media pressures to convince you that investing in the peace and clarity of your home is not as viable as investing in the outside world. In today's world, where success is often measured by external achievements, it's crucial not to underestimate the power of creating a nurturing environment within our own homes. Let not the clamor of societal pressures diminish the sanctity of homemaking.

In today's world, where success is often measured by external achievements, it's crucial not to underestimate the power of creating a nurturing environment within our own homes. Let not the noise of societal pressures diminish the sanctity of homemaking.

True fulfillment comes from living authentically according to your own values and priorities. The decision to prioritize the well-being of your home and family is a testament to your strength, compassion, and dedication. It is a choice rooted in love and nurturing, which are invaluable contributions to creating a harmonious and fulfilling life. So, embrace your role as a homemaker with pride and confidence, knowing that your efforts are meaningful and worthy of admiration. Your home is your sanctuary, and investing in its peace and clarity is a beautiful expression of self-love and care.

The four walls of your home are filled with tranquility because of you - so understanding you are blessed enough to live a life of slow mornings, clarity and peace is just as fulfilling as those sharing their ambitions to become the next CEO. I know not many people give you the credit you deserve and choosing the path of a homemaker may not seem as success orientated as climbing the corporate ladder, but homemaking does deserve a place of recognition. It's not just about rearranging furniture or decorating rooms; it's about creating an environment for your family to thrive, requiring patience, determination, and endless dedication. In the simplicity of creating a nurturing environment lies the true magic of homemaking. It's about transforming a house into a home—a sanctuary where hearts find refuge and souls find solace.

Amidst the chaos of the world, let us cherish the sacred art of homemaking, where every touch is imbued with care, every detail reflects intention, and every moment is a testament to the beauty of simplicity. If taking care of your home brings you peace and fulfillment, then that is a noble path worth embracing. Society may often glorify external achievements and career success, but true fulfillment comes from living authentically according to one's own values and priorities.

The decision to prioritize the well-being of your home and family is a testament to your strength, compassion, and dedication. It is a choice rooted in love and nurturing, which are invaluable contributions to creating a harmonious and fulfilling life. So, embrace your role as a homemaker with pride and confidence, knowing that your efforts are meaningful and worthy of admiration. Your home is your sanctuary, and investing in its peace and clarity is a beautiful expression of self-love and care.

I know not many people give you the credit you deserve, and choosing the path of a homemaker may not seem as success oriented as climbing the corporate ladder. The art of homemaking is such an undervalued role, but in its subtlety lies its strength, tranquility, and endless love. This is your reassurance that you are doing incredible things.

It's so important to heal and cleanse yourself first. Please don't feel guilty if you need to cancel a business meeting for a massage or to put yourself first by grabbing a coffee. it's so important to cherish and take care of yourself without feeling guilty. Why is the guilt there? Because you see others succeeding? Because you feel behind? If you're devoting everything to yourself, you're already way further ahead.

Your biggest asset is time. Many others wish they had the luxury of time; you've been blessed with endless time to work on yourself, on your business and you should start leveraging this to your advantage. Whether its your self-love advantage or for your business.

The universe is taking care of you; you just must take care of yourself first. And slowly but surely, you'll be attracting and finding yourself in situations that bring out the softness in you – you won't be finding yourself in survival modes. You're going to be so loved and appreciated once you love yourself.

the relaxed woman – a soft life

My love, look at you. You are the epitome of soft. You may have had a tough year or a tough season, but the fact you're here reading this is proof you are far greater than the external circumstances that made you forget who you are. You have the entire universe within you – endless potential lies at the core of your fingertips – the world is your oyster. You have everything and you always will.

You manifest everything with ease; things always work out for you; they always have and they always will. You may feel as though the universe is against you but that couldn't be farther from the truth; the universe adores you hence all the blessings around you. Your ability to love, your ability to be loved.

the relaxed woman – a soft life

You have so much goodness to offer the world; you don't even need to think twice before helping others and that's what triggers people, that's what annoys those who want to see you fail. They hate how good you are, they hate how soft you are. they hate seeing you do good in this world. But they don't know your purpose and they don't need to know. You are here to make this world the bestest place possible and if you do that by paying for someone's coffee or if you build a well in a third-world country people are always going to have something to say and that's why you must keep in tune with your greatest purpose – to help and serve others.

Seeking external validation will lead to your downfall; often, when people hear what my husband does for work they say 'oh wow, you got yourself a doctor but they fail to understand that I was the one who stood by him whilst he was becoming who he is. I was the one who stuck by him when he had nothing.

but I eventually realized not to seek this validation from others; it became frustrating for me because only one person out of everyone I know congratulated me for his success.

I absolutely do take credit for the man he is, I'm the one who stood by him through his highest and lows during his years of hard work. I was the good woman that endured the patience of him becoming the great man he was forever meant to be.

And just because women like us are so incredibly rare to find it doesn't mean we don't exist. It doesn't mean we're not out here waiting to find someone and to build with him. And those who have absolutely no willpower to do so are the ones trying to take the good women down. The ones who would never have the patience to stand by a man and help him grow and succeed are now envious of the treatment the good woman is getting for devoting this time to him. The ones trying to take from the patient girl but little do they know that patient women are rewarded and those who envy them will always receive the karma they deserve.

Some of us are still living a Godly life and all we require in return is for someone to lead. God only requires one thing from man for his wife and that is to lead. To lead with love, protection, and guidance.

A truly feminine woman understands that men and women are inherently different; she provides tranquility in times of distress; she was always supposed to be the enchanting woman cultivating a sense of peace and cooperation in her home.

the relaxed woman – a soft life

Allowing herself to be soft in all areas of life; choosing to be a soft woman at her very essence; competitiveness isn't her forte; she's so in alignment with her higher self—she's led by grace. Understanding what womanhood was to her, and once she truly understood her innate womanhood, they were left in awe of her presence.

and in the highest trajectory, she embraced wanting to make change; she truly engulfed herself in wanting to be the best version of herself.

I'm so sorry if you look back and miss the girl you once were. The memories of how incredible and warm life was for you and I'm sorry if that makes you sad – but I hope you know you have complete capability to become her or a much better version of her again. Everything you're experiencing right now is meant to happen exactly the way its playing out. Whether you find yourself in a complete opposite position to where you wish you were, whatever is happening right now in your life is happening exactly how it was supposed to. I know it's difficult to see right now but you are learning and growing whilst on this journey. I know you're tired of protecting yourself, and fighting for yourself but God is telling you to leave it with him. He is telling you; you no longer need to be on defense. Take this as your sign. you have complete capability to change your life and to begin being the soft girl you once were or the soft girl you envision becoming, you can start by speaking kindly to yourself. you can begin by taking a deep breath and surrendering. the power to become the best version of yourself is in your hands; day by day you're re-aligning; don't try and find yourself; you're en route to finding your better self.

the relaxed woman – a soft life

The guidance of her heart, the guidance of her lord has allowed her to surrender and just be and at the core of her heart, softness found itself a home. She understands that life is not about being hardworking - becoming a relaxed woman is understanding to work with ease and not to force anything. It's not to sit and not do anything but to be guided by the universe; to see everything as a sign and to simply flow. To talk to the universe for it's always there to guide. It's the one friend you can always call upon. And that's a true relaxed woman; she understands living in her purpose is what is required first. To truly attract all the wonderful things in life she needs to surrender. She's always trusted her creator; alignment is the secret. She's always been beyond her time.

the relaxed woman – a soft life

A pure woman is so in tune with her femininity that her intuition is so on point. The accuracy of her intuition is unmatched; it resembles her pure nature. She just understands how the universe works; she understands its secrets and just wishes to share them with the world. Many people want a soft life but very little understand the first step of living a truly authentic soft life begins with surrendering it to God. Allowing him to take control of every aspect of your life is the very first step to being soft.

the relaxed woman – a soft life

Many people want a soft life but very little understand the first step of living a truly authentic soft life begins with surrendering it to God. Allowing him to take control of every aspect of your life is the very first step to being soft.

They try and convince her she's 'out of touch' with the world. That her dreams are 'unrealistic' that she dreams of this life that is 'unattainable.' No baby. That life is unattainable for you not her. Her creator has so much destined for her. Just because you have a small mind that doesn't mean your beliefs should be projected upon her. Eventually, she realized that her dreams were never too high or out of touch; she was just being told this from people with no dreams at all.

the relaxed woman – a soft life

Imagine being a woman lead through her purpose and those with such little direction are having a say on how you live your life. How silly can you be to allow such small minds to have any say on your way of living. Do you understand how much you undermine yourself by surrounding yourself with such small minds?

We're not letting you do that again okay; never again am I letting you go back into that position where you're left questioning your purpose because of these small minds. No more letting people have a say on how you live your life; no more worrying and crying over their opinions, if they're more concerned with your way of living than fixing their own issues then that's on them. Let them waste their time, you keep thriving. The fact you're even reading this is the very first step. I'm proud of you for getting here but the journey to your softest life begins with commitment; being committed to bettering yourself, its what you're feeding your mind daily, your ability to stay true to yourself and working on your inner peace.

And so, she learned that the best way to stop projection of limiting beliefs was to kindly stop the conversation and place respectable boundaries so she could protect the peace of her home. The peace that mattered the most.

the relaxed woman – a soft life

My angelic girl, no more crying for you. We're going to pick ourselves back up. We're going to get up, wash our face, wash our hair, do our skincare, eat something nourishing or soothing, we're going to take our supplements that do wellness for our bodies and we're going to take ourselves out for a matcha or a coffee. Bring a book if you wish or a notepad and pen. Write a letter to the universe filled with all the things you want for the new year. Don't think about anybody else. Don't worry about anyone else. Every second is an opportunity to step into a new beginning and it's never too late to bring change upon you. We're finally channelling our inner femininity. We're surrendering and allowing God to take control. We're listening to our intuition; we're not going to allow our guilt for not responding to certain texts phase us. God will heal wounded relationships in his own timing. It's about time you start focusing on yourself. I want you to focus on what you want. Not from the perspective of a mother, a wife or anything else. I want you to see yourself as an individual first. Only then can you truly live your life as your highest self once you see yourself as whole on your own then through the purpose of serving others.

the relaxed woman – a soft life

A soft life comes to women who aren't revengeful; it comes to those who have trust in their Lord to take over and do His thing. A soft life comes to women who create an environment for their family and loved ones to thrive. It comes to those with ambition and grace.

the relaxed woman – a soft life

My sweet girl, just take a look at how soft you are. Look at how you treat people around you. If anyone has made you feel less than for the way you are - if all you do is radiate kindness and positivity - it's important to understand who to stay away from. If being kind is your purpose, you have such a magnificent life you're beyond blessed. But if anyone has ever made you question your worth or even if your etiquette and kindness has been questioned, it's important to reanalyze who you spend time with, who you give access to.

the relaxed woman – a soft life

Make it your mission to make yourself the proudest. Women like you are so rare; your mindset leaves people in awe of your existence - you're simply magnetic. Your creator has so much in store for you; your life is magical. Life is truly magical, and it's about time you begin feeling it again.

the relaxed woman – a soft life

You are one of the purest women to have ever stepped foot on this earth; you're the purest of them all. You've never lowered your boundaries and your promises to God for nobody; and you don't allow the influences of impure people and their thoughts to affect your life. Do you know how powerful that is? I don't think you understand how pure you really are; so please, next time anyone who doesn't vibrate as high as you has something to say about the way you live your life, turn to God. Sometimes you just have to give it to God and go to sleep. He'll take care of it all.

the relaxed woman – a soft life

In a world full of wounds and temptations, you are the most sacred of them all, a beacon of hope amidst the chaos, a sanctuary for weary souls seeking solace and redemption. A secure woman isn't worrying about how her creator has made her; she's embodying her flaws and finding beauty in all faults; she's committed to making her aura and energy the most beautiful things about her. Of course, they attempted to take her down; she is one of the securest women you will ever encounter. You are one of the purest women to have ever stepped foot on this earth; you're the purest of them all. You've never lowered your boundaries and your promises to God for nobody, and you don't allow the influences of impure people and their thoughts to affect your life. Do you know how powerful that is? I don't think you understand how pure you really are; so please, next time anyone who doesn't vibrate as high as you has something to say about the way you live your life, turn to God. Sometimes you just have to give it to God and go to sleep. He'll take care of it all. A relaxed woman understands the laws of the universe; she understands all she needs to do is simply relax, ask and all her blessings will flow towards her; she understands the propaganda of the world does nothing to try to misalign her from who she truly is. She embraces her uniqueness in the world even if she isn't accepted by those around her; she was never created to be average and that's why she's never fit in.

It's time to become who you've always dreamt of being. You have complete capability within to be your highest self.

God put that dream within you for a reason. Modesty lies within her core; she resists temptation and stays true to the promises she made to herself and God. Femininity wasn't her weakness; it was her greatest asset and superpower.

What people think of you doesn't take away from your worthiness from within; you are so respected and valued, my love. All you have to do is look around and see how blessed you are.

the relaxed woman – a soft life

A relaxed woman needs to go through her era of transformation, and this may require a season of screaming, pain, and agitation. But when she reaches that stage of calmness, she's truly surrendered to her Lord. She feels peace within herself, she no longer tries where her efforts weren't appreciated; she's only focused on pleasing herself from now on. After your season of pain, agitation, and screaming, you owe it to yourself to begin being kind to yourself.

the relaxed woman – a soft life

She sat and begged God to heal her heart; she didn't know why she was experiencing what she was – she had her year of confusion but decided it was time to take back her power; her soul was tired of not trusting in her Lord.

And God whispered in her ear 'I've never given you a reason not to trust me.'

patience is always rewarded; with patience comes trust, and as you step fourth into your divine embodiment of the softest version of yourself.

And despite it all, she never lost faith in her Lord.

Your creator has so much in store for you; your life is magical. Life is truly magical and it's about time you begin feeling it again.

You've always been a warrior though; you've never fitted in, so you can't exactly be surprised when suddenly things don't go your way when it comes to fitting in. I understand it's something you probably wanted and you're disappointed, but just know everything He does is for a greater purpose; He heard conversations you're unaware of. He knew you were always destined for greatness. Do you understand why there is such a strong reaction towards you? Do you understand why you've never fit in with those around you, why people always have a problem with you even though you're such a kind soul? Because nothing about you is relatable; nothing about you is relatable. And you know what? Embrace that. Because you weren't created to be average; you weren't created to fit in; you were never created to be relatable. She was always made to be different. He placed you on this earth to be extraordinary. Your path is much greater than those who have tried to diminish your light; you were just around.

the relaxed woman – a soft life

Do you understand why there is such a strong reaction towards you, do you understand why you've never fit in with those around you, why people always have a problem with you even though you're such a kind soul? because nothing about you is relatable; nothing about you is relatable. And you know what, embrace that. Because you weren't created to be average, you weren't created to fit in; you were never created to be relatable.
she was always made to be different. He placed you on this earth to be extraordinary.

the relaxed woman – a soft life

Oh, but remember how untouchable you are; you're untouchable by their words, their thoughts, their actions. Stay in your body. Keep your energy to you. Learning to preserve her energy became a priority; she was tired of giving low vibrational efforts access to her power by telling them her plans. She learned through the hard way, but she realized it was the way God had intended for her to learn. And that's how you remain magnetic.

These people who have been horrible to you don't deserve the energy you're sending out to them. And yes, by thinking about what's happened, you're sending your energy towards them. They don't deserve access to such divine resources.

She refused to grant undeserving individuals access to her divine energy, preserving her resources for those worthy of her greatness.

the relaxed woman – a soft life

It's amusing how they believe they can unsettle a woman so divinely shielded in all aspects of life. With her purity, God instructs His angels to exert extra effort to safeguard her. Should you even entertain the notion of causing her harm, I'd advise praying for your own protection, as karma has a way of evening the scales. And when her triumph arrives, it will be met with recognition and acknowledgment. She flourishes while you remain stagnant, contemplating your futile attempts. Each advancement she makes leaves you trailing behind, unable to fathom the depth of her resilience. Protected by forces unseen, she strides forward, her purity serving as both armor and weapon. So, if you ever entertained thoughts of thwarting her progress, be prepared for the consequences. As she ascends, enveloped in grace and guided by divine intervention, she leaves behind the shadows of doubt and envy. Your schemes pale in comparison to her unwavering resolve, and as she garners admiration and reverence, you're left to grapple with your own inadequacies.

the relaxed woman – a soft life

Only the misaligned are the ones trying to take away from the girl who has it all; they lack so much fulfillment in their own lives they try and take from the girl they know has the world at her fingertips; she's set herself up for greatness and put every boundary in place to become the greatest version of herself and to set the standards high for her and the family that comes from her. Nobody can come in between you and the blessings God has in store for you. And when you think about what they've done and you dwell, your creator gets sad because your only job on this earth is to simply trust. it's to trust in his timing, it's to trust all that he places in your life. Do you think they like how high you value yourself? Do you think they get happy when you walk into a room and turn heads with all your clothes on? The sooner you realize people's intentions and how to become mysterious, the better. Your purpose is much greater than what those people who tried to take you down could even fathom for themselves. So, take this time to re-find your purpose. A relaxed woman needs to go through her era of transformation, and this may require a season of screaming, pain, and agitation. But when she reaches that stage of calmness, she's truly surrendered to her Lord. She feels peace within herself, she no longer tries where her efforts aren't appreciated; she's only focused on pleasing herself from now on.

the relaxed woman – a soft life

Such a vibrant being with a sacred soul, and you expect to be loved by those with such little purity in their hearts.

the relaxed woman – a soft life

You've always had such class and grace; you cannot expect to fit in with a group that lacks the sophistication and elegance that define your innate sense of refinement.
Your self-worth surpasses their shallow perceptions; you're destined for greatness amidst their impurity.

the relaxed woman – a soft life

The sacred woman is a beacon of light, illuminating the paths of those around her with kindness and compassion. Her value transcends material wealth or status; it lies in her ability to uplift and inspire. She extends the same warmth and respect to the janitor as she does to the CEO, recognizing the inherent dignity in every individual. Her heart knows no bounds when it comes to generosity, and her success is measured not by comparison but by her own growth and evolution. Instead of viewing others as adversaries, she sees them as allies on the journey of self-improvement. Their achievements serve as reminders of the endless possibilities that await, igniting her drive to excel and make a difference. In her presence, people feel seen, heard, and valued, for she understands that true greatness lies in lifting others up, not tearing them down. She embodies the essence of a high-value woman, radiating grace, humility, and an unwavering commitment to making the world a better place.

the relaxed woman – a soft life

She takes care of everyone around her; even if it's a new group of people; she makes sure everyone on that table is okay. She embodies her femininity through her grace and her values. She's always been different and offered her grace wherever she is; often, it gets taken for granted, but she knows who she is. She has the purest of intentions and shows up wonderfully.

God blessed her because of the way she blesses others; your goal should be to become the softest version of yourself; because once you embody her, everything will fall into place.

the relaxed woman – a soft life

And so, she took back her energy and made herself into the best possible version of herself. And in the highest version of herself, she manifested everything she ever desired; God had to put her through so much emotion so she could evolve into the absolute highest version of her; and only then could she have her home; the one she was always destined for

And she made her goal to begin radiating again; begin radiating so high that absolutely nobody could ever interfere with her high vibe. She's upgrading in silence.

And in the highest version of herself she manifested everything she ever desired; God had to put her through so much emotion so she could evolve into the absolute highest version of her; and only then could she have her home; the one she was always destined for.

I need you to breathe. I need you to be okay with not knowing how things will play; sometimes it's okay to just trust.

There are so many people who wanted to see you fail this year - this may have caused you to go into your season of hibernation - away from everyone and that's okay. It's completely okay to separate yourself from energies that do not wish well upon you. But during your period of hibernation, I hope you're working on yourself. I hope you're rejuvenating your mind; I hope you're cleansing your body and your space. I hope you're letting go of energies that no longer hold importance to you, and in doing so, not only do you begin to physically glow again, but you make sure the next time they see you, they'll have to get to know you all over again. Leaving them in awe of who you've become - proving people wrong and making success your biggest revenge are all going to be your best friends during this process. Remember, the journey of self-improvement is not just about the external changes but also about the internal growth. Embrace the solitude, allow it to be your cocoon of transformation. And as you work on yourself, let resilience be your armor, determination be your guide, and self-love be your foundation. Every step you take towards personal development is a step away from the negativity that sought to bring you down. Your hibernation is not a retreat but a preparation for the comeback that will leave them in awe of your existence. So, continue to invest in your well-being, nurture your dreams, and let the echoes of their doubt fuel your journey. The next chapter of your life is not just about success; it's about becoming the person you were destined to be.

the relaxed woman – a soft life

Do you think they like how high you value yourself? Do you think they get happy when you walk into a room and turn heads with all your clothes on? The sooner you realize people's intentions and how to become mysterious, the better. Your purpose is much greater than what those people who tried to take you down could even fathom for themselves. So, take this time to re-find your purpose.

And when you re-emerge, spread your wings wide and soar higher than they ever thought you could. Prove every one of them - every one of them that wanted you to fail - wrong. Your transformation will be the greatest testament to your strength, resilience, and ability to rise above the negativity. Let success be the sweetest revenge, and let the world witness the incredible metamorphosis that is uniquely and beautifully you. Who you are at your core. I pray you never lose sight of your excellence again.

Should that happen I think it was always God's plan for you. It was His plan to help you rejuvenate yourself and control your mind; for you to always come back to your best self. He knew you needed to go on your journey of self-love again, so understand everything you're experiencing was always written to be this way.

the relaxed woman – a soft life

The moment you begin surrounding yourself with people who don't value you, you'll begin seeing yourself through their light. Stop making yourself small for those with a strong desire to diminish your light. How do you expect them to value and respect you when they don't even have this love towards themselves?

She took back her power by understanding she never actually wanted the approval of those with their character anyway. To truly embrace her soft girl life, God had to put her through a plethora of transformations first. Anyone who aspires to be in her soft girl era must understand that to thrive in such a phase, the vital ingredient is faith. It's about understanding that it's okay not to be in control all the time, that it's okay to surrender to the divine and continue with your day. It's about trusting that everything will work out for you, and understanding that, regardless of what happens, God always has your back. This transformation won't occur all at once; it'll take months of patience, healing, and commitment. Yet, when you reach a stage where you feel as though you're simply floating through life, you'll truly be free. In this soft life, there's a foundational knowledge that men are a necessity. To fully embrace your inner soft woman, it's fundamental to understand the value of men. They bring a unique strength, support, and companionship that enriches the human experience. A soft woman doesn't worry; she knows the men in her life are here to provide strength, support, and companionship. Whether that's her father, her brother, or her husband - she understands men are a necessity in life, contributing to the harmonious balance that defines a soft and fulfilling existence.

the relaxed woman – a soft life

And so, she regained her power by recognizing all her soul needed was peace; her soul simply craves a peaceful life with ease and abundance. Abundance not just in the form of wealth but an amplitude of abundance through the feeling of contentment and gratitude. She never wanted a man who had it all; she was ready to build everything together, that's how soft she was. All she ever wanted was someone in his masculine ready to put her first, and her femininity would take over.

And that's why she can provide for herself and her home, that's why she makes her house a home, that's why she can love herself and her children the way she does and that's why she's assured she will have it all because she has faith. Her faith came from finding herself, finding herself came from choosing herself and choosing herself came from losing herself. And that's when she learned life is all about an endless cycle of events that help souls become better versions of themselves. Whatever 'hurdles' may come her way, encourage growth and divinity within herself. She's now obsessed with the woman she's becoming and more unstoppable than ever. All because of the strength in her faith. We are all here for our own unique purpose, so, whether a certain individual has done things before you or whether they are experiencing more than you are, it does not matter. Train yourself to be happy for others when they succeed because ultimately, we are all on our own paths, and we are working at our own pace. Once you have mastered this concept of being genuinely happy for others' success, not only will you notice how much you are at peace with yourself, but the amount of faith you have developed in the universe will become evident. We have our own unique experiences, and each path is different.

the relaxed woman – a soft life

Respect and kindness were at the essence of her soul; if you ever found her behaving 'out of character', it's because she was never around people who were good for her soul. Her soul craved those who nourished it. And so, she became a mysterious woman, private with all her goals and ideas. And so, she learned a private life would lead her to the happiest version of herself. She was beautiful without even showing her face. Her exterior beauty was simply a reflection of the beauty within, illuminated by her kindness, compassion, and inner strength. Her mysterious aura drew people in, enticing them to uncover the depths of her soul rather than focusing solely on outward appearances. In solitude, she found solace, embracing the freedom that came with guarding her heart and dreams. Her private world became a sanctuary where she could nurture her aspirations and cultivate her innermost desires without distraction or interference. With each step taken away from the spotlight, she discovered a newfound sense of peace and authenticity, unburdened by the expectations and judgments of others. It was in the quiet moments of self-reflection that she truly blossomed, embracing her true essence and embracing the beauty of her soul.

Some people will always jump to conclusions. That serves them and spreads lies even if they're far from the truth because that's convenient for them. But you have to use their energies to transform their projections into your power to benefit you. Allow this to make you soft. Allow their bitterness towards you to transform yourself into the softest version of you. God knows what lies at the essence of your heart and that is what matters the most.

;

Some people will always jump to conclusions. That serves them and spreads lies even if they're far from the truth because that's convenient for them. But you have to use their energies to transform their projections into your power to benefit you.

the relaxed woman – a soft life

he's happiest when focused on her own; she's empowered by new ventures and doing her thing to thrive. She works best away from entities trying to take her down.

the relaxed woman – a soft life

Oh, but to become a soft woman she went through an era of pain, healing, and sacrifice – she emerged from wanting to take over the world to yearning to be the best homemaker. Being in her soft-girl era isn't just about how she dresses but how she shows up in the world; how her warmth is felt the moment she walks into a room, how she makes people feel. But what does being in your softest version mean? She's in her soft girl era – unafraid to be herself – unafraid to sit alone. She freely lives her life; she floats through life with ease.

from wanting to take over the world to yearning to be the best homemaker
And so, day by day, she began nurturing herself; eventually, she became the unstoppable girl with a heart full of grace and a soul filled with love.

the relaxed woman – a soft life

I want you to go back to being the girl who lives her life through the lens of appreciation and gratitude, for your Lord has blessed you with such a wonderful life, and you owe it to Him to feel again.

Choosing to be a homemaker is just as commendable as climbing the corporate ladder. Please do not allow the influx of social media pressures to convince you that investing in the peace and clarity of your home is not as viable as investing in the outside world. In today's world, where success is often measured by external achievements, it's crucial not to underestimate the power of creating a nurturing environment within our own homes. True fulfilment comes from living authentically according to your own values and priorities. The decision to prioritize the well-being of your home and family is a testament to your strength, compassion, and dedication. It is a choice rooted in love and nurturing, which are invaluable contributions to creating a harmonious and fulfilling life. So, embrace your role as a homemaker with pride and confidence, knowing that your efforts are meaningful and worthy of admiration. Your home is your sanctuary, and investing in its peace and clarity is a beautiful expression of self-love and care. The four walls of your home are filled with tranquility because of you - so understanding you are blessed enough to live a life of slow mornings, clarity, and peace is just as fulfilling as those sharing their ambitions to become the next CEO. I know not many people give you the credit you deserve, and choosing the path of a homemaker may not seem as success oriented as climbing the corporate ladder, but homemaking deserves endless recognition. In the simplicity of creating a nurturing environment lies the true magic of homemaking. It's about transforming a house into a home—a sanctuary where hearts find refuge and souls find solace. Amidst the chaos of the world, let us cherish the sacred art of homemaking, where every touch is imbued with care, every detail reflects intention, and every moment is a testament to the beauty of simplicity. If taking care of your home brings you peace and fulfilment, then that is a noble path worth embracing. Society may often glorify external achievements and career success, but true fulfilment comes from living authentically according to one's own values and priorities. The decision to prioritize the well-being of your home and family is a testament to your strength, compassion, and dedication. It is a choice rooted in love and nurturing, which are invaluable contributions to creating a harmonious and fulfilling life. So, embrace your role as a homemaker with pride and confidence, knowing that your efforts are meaningful and worthy of admiration. Your home is your sanctuary, and investing in its peace and clarity is a beautiful expression of self-love and care. I know not many people give you the credit you deserve, and choosing the path of a homemaker may not seem as success oriented as climbing the corporate ladder. The art of homemaking is an undervalued role, but in its subtlety lies its strength, tranquility, and endless love. This is your reassurance that you are doing incredible things.

the relaxed woman – a soft life

I am so sorry if you've been made to feel less than, especially if this was from someone whom you once valued. This is your reminder that you have complete capability to take control and action to change how you feel. Nobody should have the power to ruin your day unless you give it to them. Your self-worth isn't defined by what others think of you, it isn't defined by how they've made you feel; the only person who has the power to define you is you - how you show up to the world despite their efforts to try and take you down.

the relaxed woman – a soft life

You are *that* girl, and you must believe you are that girl; your energy is so magnetic; the entire room is left in awe of you; your presence is so powerful people want to take you down. If you were a nobody, do you think they'd be trying?

And I pray you reach a sense of peace within yourself, where your screams and hardness are eradicated, and one day you are going to be so loved; you are going to have everything. Extraordinary power lies within you; extraordinary power lies within your faith.

.

Her path is more difficult because her calling was much greater than one could ever imagine.

And God said to her, "Trust in me, my angelic girl; that's all you'll ever have to do. If I taught you anything last year it was to trust in me and only me. No exterior entity. If you have faith in me, I will always make sure your soul receives whatever it needs. And what do I mean by having faith in me? Stop focusing on things that are out of your control; your happiness is always at my core; stop thinking about external entities that have ever let you down and consequently made you anxious; you should trust in me and if you trust that I've never given you any reason not to believe in me then just breathe and let life happen the way it's supposed to. Your job on earth is to amplify the beauty around you and all you need to do is breathe, give back to the world in your own way and simply just trust. I will always work things out for you. Just like I always have. Stop thinking about things that haven't put you first. The only thing that's ever supposed to put you first is me. I'll never wrong you. I created you. I put you here your happiness is my job. Your only job is to put your complete trust in me. Do you trust in me my angelic girl?"

the relaxed woman – a soft life

Your life is not the opinions or thoughts of others; it's what I have in store for you. As your creator, I will work things out for you. I will give your soul everything it needs for its nourishment and your energy to thrive. Only me. Your job is to simply put your trust in me. Your complete trust.

The soul knows what it wants, and the soul knows exactly what it needs to experience. So just know everything happening in your life is happening exactly as it should be. Your soul knows what path it needs to take to live its purpose; to fulfill the reasons why it chose to bring you forth into this world.

the relaxed woman – a soft life

She's fully aware anything she's lost she was never supposed to have; any person she's lost, her soul had simply seen enough of them. Her soul outgrew them because she was always here for a much higher purpose.

Those who have ever tried to destroy what you have don't understand how protected you are; they don't realize how much God adores you; those who are maliciously trying to speak badly about your name have no idea what's coming. So I urge you to continue working on yourself; allow God to control everything. Your life is so special, so stop being sad about these people who seem to be obsessed and have something to say about your every move and how you choose to live your life. Think about that for a minute, it only takes a miserable and unfulfilled person to sit there and try to re-evaluate your life instead of trying to focus and upgrade from their mistakes. It takes a troubled soul to criticize, but you, my love, are on a journey of self-discovery and growth. So, for now, focus on healing and upgrading. I hope amidst this all you have learned how to impose boundaries; boundaries where you are happy to end a conversation if you feel there is a malicious emotion behind their questioning; listen to your intuition.

I think sometimes you forget how powerful you are. You are so elevated in life; you are such a powerful woman with endless blessings awaiting her arrival – more than any of these people can even imagine for themselves. Stop betraying that little girl in you and start by giving her the love she deserves. You truly deserve to start being kind to yourself again – nobody else's opinions matter. I promise you that. When you begin to have a higher sense of self-worth, you will not care.

the relaxed woman – a soft life

And as you cultivate a higher sense of self-worth, the annoyance of others' opinions will fade into insignificance. And I understand that this is easier said than done, but truly understand this, where do you see yourself in five years? I can assure you; you'll be further ahead than any of these people trying to bring you down. Amidst the chaos of the world, your resilience speaks volumes. If people still attempt to snatch from your essence, recognize it simply as a testament to your victories.

When you're God's favorite, nobody else's opinions can bring you down. When you're God's favorite, you live your life with ease and flow. You go about feeling protected, nourished, and knowing you're always being taken care of. When you're God's favorite, a higher power takes care and control. You radiate graciousness wherever you go; when you're God's favorite, the weight of societal judgments and opinions becomes inconsequential. The world's standards no longer define your worth, for you are guided by a divine purpose and shielded by a higher power. In the face of criticism or disapproval, you remain steadfast, knowing that you are cherished by something far greater than the approval of others. When you know you're God's favorite, why must you care that you're the least favored in a certain room? He's given you blessings upon blessings. When you know you're God's favorite, you walk through life with ease; you embrace your faults and simply just rise. Embracing your faults and imperfections becomes an integral part of your journey. Instead of being weighed down by self-doubt, you rise above challenges with the certainty that you are God's favorite. This knowledge becomes a source of strength, resilience, and unwavering self-love. So, walk through life with ease, knowing that you are God's favorite, always. Embrace the unique path that unfolds before you, for you are divinely guided and protected. In this realization, find the strength to be true to yourself and to live authentically. Just know you're God's favorite, always.

You have such a magnificent life; you're beyond blessed. Women like you are so rare; your mindset leaves people in awe of your existence - you're simply magnetic. Your creator has so much in store for you; your life is magical. Life is truly magical, and it's about time you begin feeling it again. Remember to always do things for yourself. Remember to always take time for yourself. Remember to cherish your own company again.

Becoming a magnetic woman is about embracing the privileges of hosting soft mornings, feeling entirely detached from what people have to say or think about you, and putting your mind on 'do not disturb'. It's about keeping your energy inward so nobody can feed off you while staying connected to the source, aiming to be the best version of yourself. It's about keeping your focus and energy inward, creating the woman you want to be, and understanding that so much can happen in a year—look at how much has changed, how much you have grown in the space. Becoming limitless in your mind means separating yourself from the norm's society has created for us, understanding that your worth isn't determined by productivity or external opinions. if your vision is to be a lady of leisure, take care of your home, be a housewife, have slow mornings, it's about embracing your desires without shame in a world consumed by hustle culture. Inspire fellow women to take life easy and be the breath of fresh air this world needs.

the relaxed woman – a soft life

To be soft, feminine, and gracious while embracing your uniqueness is key, understanding that you are more than enough in all that you do. It's about doing the inner work and not caring about exterior opinions, stopping the fear of judgment from holding you back from becoming your best version—a warrior who conquers fears and lives authentically.

Being a woman of power means loving and accepting yourself for who you are, cherishing your body, and the aura you emit. You're naturally feminine and seek approval from nobody. So continue emitting the magnetic aura that you are; the universe will continue blessing you with endless potential.

She understands the power of her mind and the energy she emits. Taking life slow and trusting the process is one of her greatest abilities. Though she's felt lost and drained at times, she finally grasps that she alone has complete control over her feelings.

Change begins the moment you decide to take action. Even if you've lost yourself for a while, understanding that you hold the reins of your emotions is a powerful realization. Taking action to actively improve yourself is immensely underrated; the process of progress is seldom shown on social media, but the results are. It's crucial to be patient with yourself on this journey of self-discovery and growth. You've got this.

the relaxed woman – a soft life

In a field of lavender, you are a rose. Soft yet resistant, you can turn heads with all your petals. But most importantly, you're the most unique of them all. In a lavender field, you are a daisy.

the relaxed woman – a soft life

You are here worrying about people who have absolutely nothing on you. Next time you're wasting your time thinking about these people why don't you think about how to improve yourself so the next time they see you you're unrecognizable. Be so completely investing in yourself that no matter what's happening around you, your inner peace is so high vibrational nothing can ever get in the way of you and your greatness again my love.

Okay, they're talking about you? And you're here sitting and being sad about it? Get up and do some work. Work on yourself and win whilst they're doing it; that's the only way you'll win and progress. No more sadness, my angel, I know you have complete control of picking yourself back up. You're going to get through this, and you're going to find yourself; you're going to love the version of you that appears out of this consequence. You will be okay.

Again, he is one entity that has never given me a reason not to trust in him. The relaxed woman surrenders herself to God. She knows he's always got her covered. This is your reminder of the power of your faith; never underestimate it, please.

the relaxed woman – a soft life

And God whispered to her that she could finally fall asleep in peace; he told her she knew deep down in her heart he was always working things out for her. He whispered to her that everything would be alright. And it would; just like it always did and is.

Allow yourself to be loved; immerse yourself in the greatness of this world. Oh but baby, you're untouchable. You're untouchable by their words, their thoughts. Prioritizing reasonable boundaries. Stay in your body. Keep your energy to you. And that's how you remain magnetic. These people who have been horrible to you don't deserve the energy you're sending out to them. And yes, by thinking about what's happened you're sending your energy towards them. They don't deserve access to such divine resources. You are touching lives each day without even knowing your power; you have such little knowledge of your influence and power in this world.

Not having reached certain goals shouldn't require the amount of impatience you're having towards yourself. Before we came forth into this world, we knew everything; we signed an agreement that everything we're experiencing would happen, but we also knew they wouldn't defeat us. We have a purpose and everything we're going through is helping us achieve our life's purpose. Whether or not you're aware, your presence still impacts many people; whether a smile towards someone on the tube or your presence alone at a table, you have impacted more people than you know. Someone has felt warmth towards you and that is far more valuable than any other goal. One thing I'm still learning is 'it's how we deal with circumstances that lead to our quality of life' - as I write this I am still learning to surrender. I pray God remains patient with me. He is one entity that has never given me a reason not to trust in him. This year might have been the heaviest you've experienced; you might be an entirely different person you are right now than this time last year - whether it's a positive or negative that's okay. You might not even recognize the person you are anymore but remember he is transitioning you; allow him to lead you. I write in my book, 'Perspective,' 'Let the most high lead you' and I think sometimes we just need to take our own advice.

And you'll come back home to yourself; for now, you need to fill your mind with things that bring you greatness; growth opportunities; opportunities to love yourself more. The first step is to stop overstimulating your mind. Life is about doing something big for you; it's about choosing yourself over and over again; especially as women and for those of us who want to become mothers and take care of our homes, it's so important to pour into ourselves despite the opinions and distractions of others; As a woman, it's your role to protect the peace of your family and to promote harmony, and that's why it's so important to pour into yourself. In this generation, it's so easy to be distracted; so, it's important to tune into your values and who you are; and you can do this by promoting things that bring you peace; from going for a massage, having facials to drinking matcha and appreciating life.

the relaxed woman – a soft life

A relaxed woman understands the laws of the universe; she understands all she needs to do is simply relax, ask and all her blessings will flow towards her; she understands the propaganda of the world does nothing to try to misalign her from who she truly is. She embraces her uniqueness in the world even if she isn't accepted by those around her; she was never created to be average and that's why she's never fit in. She's never been relatable. She lives her life through the lens of appreciation; she was never meant to share her energy with those who find everything to complain about.

the relaxed woman – a soft life

she's one of the realest and was happy build with man. she never desired a man who had it all; she never wanted a man with everything. all she ever wanted was for her partner to fight for her and win. her creator would provide her with everything else.

the relaxed woman – a soft life

Before she walked this earth, she was destined for a soft life, deeply connected to the divine. Some may see her as 'out of touch,' but she's profoundly in tune, effortlessly manifesting blessings.

the relaxed woman – a soft life

She's the girl you'll find smiling randomly because she takes moments of appreciation to thank her Lord for everything. Her ability to sit alone and appreciate life as it goes on around her without the worry of what others think of her is one of her powerful qualities. Her inner peace is all that she requires. She owes it to her younger self to relax and be easy with life; to allow life to be life. Her inner strength is derived from her ability to trust.

Oh, but not everyone will understand you. They don't even have the same heart as you, let alone share the same values. Talk to God; he's waiting for you to call upon him.

Not everyone will understand her, but that's okay. She's chosen softness as a lasting path, transcending past hurts. She embraces pain to become her softest self, finding validation within.

And to become a soft woman she learned this wasn't just a phase, this is who she wanted to be; this version of her was going to last. You are bigger than what's hurt you and you're destined for more than who has hurt you. They know they'll never be on your level; you're so high they can't even fathom competing with you so instead they take the easy route.

and to become the softest version of her she needed an environment where she could just be. without begging, without having to ask, she just needed to be.

the relaxed woman – a soft life

And so she embraced all the experiences that caused her pain and agony, to become the softest version of herself. Her and her mind alone will take you to unimaginable places. External validation was never there; she had everything she ever needed.

the relaxed woman – a soft life

Her comfortability in her own skin was one of her greatest values; knowing her heart was the most beautiful thing about her. And to become the softest version of her she needed an environment where she could just be, without begging, without having to ask, she just needed to be.

So embraced all the experiences that caused her pain and agony, to become the softest version of herself.

Comfortable in her skin, her inner beauty shines brightest. She thrives in an environment where she can simply exist, without seeking validation or approval.

Her and her mind alone will take you to unimaginable places; she was a woman of grace.

the relaxed woman – a soft life

And so, slowly but surely, she stopped giving away her power; she became soft – she became the best possible version of herself. She learned hurting a woman like that was always going to lead to your own downfall; do you know how protected she is, how much grace her soul holds? Do you even know how high her purpose is?

Slowly, she reclaims her power, becoming her best self. Hurting her only leads to one's own downfall, for her soul is resilient and purposeful.

the relaxed woman – a soft life

hurting a woman like that was always going to lead to your own downfall; do you know how protected she is, how much grace her soul holds. do you even know how high her purpose is

the relaxed woman – a soft life

What is the meaning of this life? Why are we placed here? What lessons are we meant to learn? Why does our soul choose to come forth into this dimension? There is so much to think about. And the art of softness took over; her power lies within her presence alone. She loved seeing other women succeed because she knows how much she was destined for; seeing others succeed was simply a motivation for her to be better and do better. Others' success never took away from her own; she was always destined for much more.

Taking life advice from those so out of tune with themselves was the worst possible thing one could do – the highest vibrational entities create their own reality by listening to what's in their own heart. They know external opinions mean very little to them; they came into this world to strive upon their own path and live their own purpose – no matter who supports them and no matter who goes against them. These qualities lie at the very essence of a cycle breaker. Many of these entities are strong in their faith – they embrace their journey – whether goodness is physically appearing or whether there is a curse right in front of them – they understand everything they're experiencing is leading them to the destiny they were always meant to experience to make them into the best version of themselves.

I'm trying to find the balance between taking the little girl inside of me out of her comfort zone and helping her grow but also reminding her it's okay to wallow and take care of her soul. It's okay to take time to understand what you need - it's okay to breathe and not be too hard on yourself - rediscovering the softest version of you isn't going to be the easiest of journeys - especially if you've been in a certain dynamic for years. But in rediscovering yourself, I want you to understand things are happening exactly the way they should be. Finding a balance between embracing loss or going through a dramatic change, with taking yourself out of your comfort zone and learning will be an unpredictable journey. Still, I want you to remember that it's only within facing this messiness that we discover who we truly are at our core. It's only after this that we realize how authentic and soft we are. See this process as a rejuvenating retreat as opposed to a loss. It's the transition into a higher version of yourself and in experiencing this change, we come out the strongest; it's about embracing the infinite potential that has been lying dormant in our souls. Everything you do, do mindfully. This process will help you live your life with ease - and you deserve an easy life - things will fall into place; I know you're hurting; you're mourning - whether it's the loss of another or an older version of you - everything will be okay. Taking yourself out of your comfort zone - exploring new things - even if it's as simple as having a cold shower or journaling - constantly working on yourself. And my sweet girl many more opportunities are awaiting your presence; it's about remaining mindful and open to everything that's happening.

You'll get to that place of peace when you are supposed to. And It will all return. Your kindness will return, your softness will return, and your patience will return. You'll rediscover yourself. Come on, my angel, get yourself back up. I know you're entirely capable of amazing things. I know you don't recognize yourself right now, but you have complete power to change your destination. I know it's scary but think about the growth and the transformation. You're boundless, you're limitless, set yourself free. You will be in a much better situation, and everything will fall into place. It sure takes its precious time - but you'll get there. I know you will, and you'll be more liberated than ever.

This is your sign that it will all be okay - that rejection and starting over is okay. I've always said, 'one step back is always two steps forward' but recently I've struggled to take my own advice. I think when we've worked so hard for something and we don't get it, it is okay to wallow, it's okay to take time away but it's just as important to come back stronger; each setback presents an opportunity to learn, to adapt, and to emerge stronger and more resilient than before. With the glamorization of success on social media, not many people talk about the power of rejection and how it can be your greatest superpower - if you use it to your advantage. Rejection is your greatest asset, reaping the benefits of it often go unnoticed but when you do, you have complete capability to transform that rejection into your favor so you can benefit as though you got the actual win in the first place. But here's the thing: it's okay to wallow. It's okay to take a step back, grab a matcha, and take some time away. However, it's equally important to remember that this setback is not the end of the road. But amidst that pause, it's crucial to understand that setbacks aren't the end-all. They're merely detours in our journey— an opportunity to pause, reflect, and ultimately emerge stronger. Through setbacks, we gain valuable insights into how to improve, how to navigate challenges, and most importantly, you now know how to improve, you know how to face certain situations, and build resilience. All these tools help us on our life journey - the most important journey of them all. We often become so engulfed in the success of the outside world including our careers but those aren't the reasons why we came fourth into this world. Ultimately, what's the purpose of life? Our souls chose to come fourth so we could embrace our personal journeys to become the greatest versions of ourselves, to experience challenges, to learn, to heal to help others, and to serve. We are not our careers; we are not our businesses. Moments like these prompt us to reevaluate our core values, reminding us of who we truly are at our very essence. In a world where success is often glamorized and filtered through the lens of social media, the power of rejection is often overlooked. We rarely talk about its transformative potential, its ability to shape us into the resilient beings we were meant to be. In a world where hustle culture often prevails, there's a certain relief in granting oneself permission to pause and recharge. These things require us to embrace rejection with open arms, knowing that within its depths lie hidden treasures. As someone once said to me, 'heads or tails, you always win'. - the wisest piece of advice I've ever received. So let's start talking about rejection the way we talk about our successes. Let's celebrate the resilience it builds, the lessons it imparts, and the growth it inspires. Because when we learn to reap the benefits of rejection, we succeed in ways we never thought possible. And in the end, isn't that the true measure of victory? Isn't that what life is about? The learning curves and the journey towards becoming a better person; the tools we gather during times of setbacks are the ones that help us throughout our life journey.

Ultimately, staying true to yourself and trusting in your inherent value will lead you to greater peace and fulfilment, regardless of any external influences. If she's accomplishing great things and enjoying the best life has to offer, and you feel compelled to diminish her happiness, pause and reflect on your own aspirations.

the relaxed woman – a soft life

the relaxed woman – a soft life

Copyright © 2024 the relaxed woman

a soft life

All rights reserved.

ISBN: 978-1-914275-99-9

Perspective Press Global Ltd

Also, by Eleni Sophia

'This One's for You' a poetry collection about the power of self-love and finding oneself.

'From Ours to Yours' a collection written by Eleni Sophia & pn.writes – where the couple discuss the nonexistent honeymoon phase, interfaith, and the power of appreciation.

'Perspective by Sophia'- a motivational book, where Sophia simplifies the 'law of attraction' and encourages you on living a life that you love, just by changing your mindsets!

'Good Morning to Goodnight' the rawest collection about 'love' and first heartbreak.

'Breaking the Cycle' a collection of the power of breaking generational cycles, embracing your femininity and the beauty in balancing a career and motherhood.

the relaxed woman – a soft life

She's the type of woman you know is going to have it all. Just one look at her and you know. Not because other people believe in her, but because she believes in herself. She's the one breaking all the generational curses; she's known as the 'rule breaker and the troublemaker.' And she's okay with that. The outside noise is just noise. We often hear, 'Tradition is nothing but advice from the dead' and my goodness, how true is that?! She's forever the protector of her future home, partner, and children. And as she becomes aligned and in tune with her higher self, she embodies her truth. Clothed in self-love, filled with ambition, and protected. You'll fall in love with her magic. She knows she will have it all.
– Breaking the Cycle by Eleni Sophia

Wish them the very best And let them walk away If they don't want to be a part of your life anymore Maybe it's time for this particular journey to end. And I know it's hard It is so incredibly hard; You're left wondering what you did wrong But I urge you to shift your perspective; If you can give so much compassion to the wrong one Think about how much you will be able to give to the one meant for you. The fact that you were able to show so much emotion shows how much you can love, and that is truly magnificent.
Maybe one day you will cross paths grown and evolved
You will look back with clarity And realize why things happened
If they are meant to be in your life Inevitably, It will happen. For now, Continue to put yourself first It's finally time to start making yourself a priority Putting your happiness first. You deserve everything this world has to offer and more Learn to give it to yourself first
You will see why.
– This One's for You by Eleni Sophia

About the Publisher:

Perspective Press Global is an independent publishing firm representing authors under the age of 20.

At Perspective Press Global, our mission is to inspire young aspiring authors that there is no such thing as being 'too young;' your voices deserve to be heard.

The firm was founded based on Sophia's struggle to find representation when she was a 13-year-old writer.
We now have published young talent from around the globe – including, the UK, Albania, Kosovo, Ireland, and Australia!

If you're interested in joining our team, please visit our submissions page at perspectivepressglobal.com and come say hello over on Instagram @PerspectivePressGlobal

Signed copies of all books can be found on perspectivepressglobal.com

For Eleni Sophia's work follow @EleniiSophia

Printed in Great Britain
by Amazon